For our David Barker
Christmas 1982
Mom & Dad

For our David Barker
Christmas 1982
Mom & Dad

WHO WHAT WHEN WHERE

Book about the Bible

Holy Bible

William L. Coleman
illustrated by Dwight Walles

Chariot Books

About the Author

BILL COLEMAN graduated from Washington Bible College and Grace Theological Seminary. He has served as pastor of the North Shores Baptist Church, the Sterling Evangelical Mennonite Church, and Aurora Evangelical Free Church. Among his other books for children are: *My Magnificent Machine, More about My Magnificent Machine; Listen to the Animals; Counting the Stars;* and *On Your Mark.* His books for adults include *Understanding Suicide; A Dozen Daring Christians; Those Pharisees; Lord, Sometimes I Need Help; It's Your Funeral; The Engagement Elevator;* and *Letters from Dad.*

About the Artist

DWIGHT WALLES has illustrated other books for children, including *Santa, Are You for Real? Easter Bunny, Are You for Real? I Learn about Angels,* and *I Learn about the Bible.*

Editor: Janet Hoover Thoma

Special thanks to:
James Townsend, Ph. D.
Bible Editor
David C. Cook

WHO, WHAT, WHEN, WHERE BOOK ABOUT THE BIBLE
© 1980 David C. Cook Publishing Co.

Scripture quotations, unless otherwise noted, are from the New International Version.

Printed in the United States of America

First Edition
July 1980

Library of Congress Cataloging in Publication Data

Coleman, William L
  Who, what, when, where book about the Bible.

  (Chariot books)
  Includes index.
  SUMMARY: Contains Bible stories and facts, activity pages and answers to such questions as "Why does God allow bank robberies?"
  1. Bible games and puzzles—Juvenile literature. [1. Bible—Miscellanea. 2. Bible games and puzzles. 3. Games]
I. Title.
GV1507.B5C64   200'.7   80-66593

ISBN 0-89191-291-6

Contents

The Wonderful World of the Bible

The Bible is packed with stories of secret spies, beautiful queens, and amazing kings. There is also a talking donkey, a sun that stood still, and a fish who gave change.

Spend some time with the people who lived out this fascinating history. Learn the games they played and the sports they loved. Find out about the strange medicines they used, the cosmetics they wore, and the miracles they saw.

As you travel through this book you will find yourself learning about God and his Son. It promises to be a tremendous journey.

Were you ever embarrassed?

Have you ever felt your face turn red? Have you ever wished the floor would open up so you could crawl in?

There is a man in the Bible who must have felt just that way. He was a new Christian, and his name was Eutychus (pronounced YOU-tih-kus).

His embarrassing day came in a town called Troas. Eutychus went to hear a sermon by the famous Apostle Paul. The service was held on the third floor of a house. People packed the room and perhaps the air was stuffy. The room was so full Eutychus sat in the open window.

Paul's sermon was long. At midnight he was still preaching.

The late hour and stuffy room started to bother poor Eutychus. His eyes began closing and his eyelids became heavy as lead.

Finally he could fight it no more and went to sleep. No one noticed. Eutychus began to rock gently on the window ledge. No one noticed. He swayed backwards hanging out the window. No one noticed. *Clunk!* Eutychus fell out the window and dropped three stories like a sack of plaster.

Quickly everyone ran down the stairs and outside to see how badly he was hurt. Eutychus was dead. The Apostle Paul reached down and hugged the young man. Then Paul looked at the crowd and said, "Don't be alarmed. He's alive."

It was definitely a miracle to bring him back to life. But Eutychus must have been terribly embarrassed.

(Acts 20:7-12)

8

Are you left-handed?

If you are, you might have qualified for a special troop of soldiers.

Seven hundred men were chosen because they were left-handed. Each was given careful training in twirling and shooting a left-handed motion sling.

These slings were not toys. Historians believe they could hold a stone weighing up to one pound. They also believe a skilled slingshooter could send a stone at the incredible speed of ninety miles an hour.

In war these slingshots were frightening. They could do tremendous damage. The Bible says the soldiers in this unit could hit a target and practically never miss.

To belong to this skilled group you had to be left-handed.   (Judges 20:16)

This is especially true if God decides to chang
of how God did funny things to the sun, the b:

The Wet Wool (Judges 6:36-40)

A man named Gideon was told by God to lead an army to throw the Midianites out of Israel. Gideon asked for a sign to show him he would win.

He placed a piece of wool on the ground and left it overnight. In the morning the wool was soaked with dew, but the ground was dry. The wool was so wet Gideon wrung a bowlful of water out of it.

The Lions Wouldn't Eat (Daniel 6)

Daniel was told he could no longer bow down and pray to God. If he did, he would be arrested and killed. Danie prayed anyway, three times a day.

The king and his officials soon arres ed Daniel. He was placed in a den of lio and the stone door was sealed shut. Wh the king came to look the next morning Daniel was healthy and happy. God had closed the mouths of the lions so they wouldn't harm him.

The Fish Who Gave Change (Matthew 17:2

Tax collectors wanted to know if Jesus paid taxes or if he refused. When Peter asked Jesus, he sent Peter to the lake to bring back a fish. When he opened the fish's mouth, Peter found a coin inside. The coin was used to pay the taxes.

nd. The Bible is packed with stories
, and fish. These are a few of those stories.

The Sun Stood Still (Joshua 10)

General Joshua asked God for a strange thing. He was leading his army against the Amorites and beating them. However, it was getting dark. Joshua was afraid the enemy would get away.

The general prayed and asked God to hold the sun still. God did it. The sun did not move for about twenty-four hours.

Somehow God had to hold the earth, the sun, and the moon in one position. Sound impossible? It is—except by a miracle.

Colorful Rainbows (Genesis 9:13)

God may have made the rainbow for a specific purpose. After he flooded the earth, he promised to never do it again. He put a rainbow in the sky to remind us of his promise.

The Fire That Didn't Burn (Daniel 3)

Three Hebrew men, Shadrach, Meshach, nd Abednego, were told to worship a gold tatue. They refused because they worhiped the true God.

A fire was heated extra hot. Each of he three were tied tightly. They were hrown into the flaming, scorching, roaring fire.

God protected them in the fire. Not one hair as singed. They didn't even have a smoke mell. The fire didn't burn.

Why take things that don't belong to you?

It happens all the time. A boy takes his sister's radio. A girl borrows her sister's comb and doesn't give it back. People are happier if they give back the things that aren't theirs.

The Philistines learned this lesson the hard way. They fought the Israelites and captured the ark of God. That sounded good. Their chests were puffed out. They probably strutted around like frisky horses. "Look at what we did!"

The ark was a large, important box. It held the Ten Commandments, a pot of manna, and Aaron's rod. It was about four feet by two-and a-half feet and covered with gold.

Before long the Philistines would wish they had never seen it.

They took the captured ark to their town. It was placed inside the temple of their god, Dagon.

They were probably still strutting around. "Look what we did!"

The ark was left overnight.

When they came in to check it the next day, the statue of their idol had fallen on its face. How could that happen. It never had before. They dusted Dagon off and put him back. It must have been an accident.

The next day they came back. Poor Dagon had fallen on his face again. This time Dagon was hurting. The statue's hands and head had broken off. They dusted Dagon off again. He didn't look good. He was just a body with no head or arms.

Soon something funny started happening. People could feel little pimples on the back of their necks. The pimples grew longer. They were painful. Now the people realized these weren't pimples but ugly boils. Boils hurt and itch, but you can't scratch them. They might become infected and get worse. The people were miserable.

Before long the Philistines gave the ark back to Israel. They also threw in a large present of gold. They had learned not to keep things that didn't belong to them.
(1 Samuel 5-6, The Living Bible)

13

First, Most, And Least

Methuselah (muh-THOO-zuh-luh) was the oldest man who ever lived. He reached 969 years.

The first person killed for being a Christian was **Stephen**.

Goliath may be the tallest man. He reached over nine feet tall.

Abel was the first person murdered in the Bible. His brother, Cain, did him in.

A day's journey in Bible times was around twenty miles.

The smallest number of verses in a book of the Bible exists in 2 John. It only has **13** verses.

Peter and **John** were the first Christians jailed for their faith.

Lamech (LAY-mek) was the first man to have two wives.

The first bottles in the Bible were made from animal skins.

Balaam had the first (and maybe only) talking donkey.

Samson was probably the strongest man in the Bible. He grabbed two pillars (or posts) in the temple and brought the entire building down.

The first bird named in the Bible is the raven.

Samson tied the tails of 300 foxes in pairs and set their tails afire to burn the Philistines' wheat fields.

15

What is heaven like?

Do you have a relative who has gone to heaven? What could he be doing there? What will you do when you arrive?

Most of the things we are used to are probably not there. There are probably no bicycles or motorcycles. What if there are no record players, television sets, or pizzas? There might not even be an amusement park.

This doesn't mean heaven is dull. There is plenty to see and do. Enough to last us forever.

The Bible gives us some broad clues about what to expect. We can see the details when we get there.

Heaven is fun

When Jesus was on the earth, he enjoyed going places, meeting people, and doing things. Heaven must be filled with broad smiles and good laughs. It must be as the psalm writer said, "In thy presence is fulness of joy at thy right hand there are pleasures for evermore." (Psalm 16:11, King James Version)

Heaven is healthy

Christians have been promised strong new bodies. There won't be any casts for broken legs. No eyeglasses, hearing aids, wheelchairs, or corrective shoes. No braces (for teeth or legs), no need for vitamin pills, false teeth, or hospitals. Some of the things we can't do now we will be able to do then.

(Revelation 21:4)

Heaven is musical

What type of music will be in heaven? There will probably be large choirs, but there could also be small vocal and musical groups. What kind of instruments will there be? Pianos, guitars, organs, saxophones, drums, violins, and harmonicas? Maybe there will be instruments we have never seen before. Will the music be slow or fast? Loud or soft? Could it change from time to time?

Some of us do not sing very well. Maybe God will give us new voices, too. (Revelation 5:8,9; Revelation 19:1)

Heaven is busy

We aren't going to rest on clouds, play harps, and eat grapes. Our job in heaven will be to serve Jesus Christ. What does this mean? Will we run errands or build buildings? Maybe it will be work like we have never seen before. Whatever it is, we will enjoy serving him.

(Revelation 22:3)

Heaven is happy

No one will ever cry in heaven. The biggest reason is because there won't be anything to cry about.

There will be no more death. Everyone who gets there will stay. We won't have to see a grandparent, uncle, parent, brother, or sister die. We will be together to stay. (Revelation 21:4)

17

Heaven is friendly

It is a collection of old and new friends. We will see people we haven't seen for years. There will be relatives we have never met. We can meet Eskimos, Indians, Vikings, Chinese, Roman soldiers, and kings.

The most important person will be Christ.

(Philippians 2:10,11;
1 Thessalonians 4:17)

Heaven is closer to God

We know some things about God now, but there is much we have never understood. In heaven God will become even clearer. It will be a better life living near to God.

(1 Corinthians 15:12)

The Bible didn't say it.

We hear many stories that aren't true. For years people have said the Bible teaches things that it doesn't. Here's your chance to get the facts straight.

The Bible *did not* say these things:

The Bible does *not* say Eve sinned by eating an apple off a tree. It says she ate a fruit.

The Bible does *not* say Goliath was killed by a stone from David's sling. He was knocked unconscious by the stone. David then killed Goliath with his own sword.

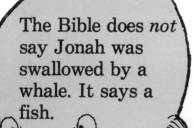

The Bible does *not* say money is the root of all evil. It says the love of money is the root of all kinds of evil.

The Bible does *not* say Jonah was swallowed by a whale. It says a fish.

The Bible does *not* say all animals came to Noah in twos. Some came in sevens.

The Bible does *not* say there were three wisemen who visited the baby Jesus. It only names three gifts they brought and doesn't number the men.

Riddles

Moses

No need to fear,
Just keep near.
He'll make the waters
Disappear.
(Exodus 14:15-28)

Here's a mystery,
Suspense sublime.
Who turned water
Into wine?
(Luke 2:1-11)

Jesus

Tell me if you can,
Tell me if you dare,
Who wore a suit
Made from camel hai
(Matthew 3:4)

I hope he likes the toothy tiger,
Giraffe, panda, and goat.
I hope he likes them living close
While floating on a boat.
(Genesis 6-7)

Noah

A lot of people like
you and me
Will never grow
extraordinarily.
When there was something
special to see,
He had to climb
a sycamore tree.

(Luke 19:1-10)

John the Baptist

Zacchaeus

You don't have to be rich
To be strong, kind, and able.
The best person ever
Started in a stable.

(Luke 2:4-6)

Jesus

21

Too Many Soldiers

When Gideon went to war against the Midianites, he sent out a call for soldiers. Quickly 32,000 men volunteered.

Gideon felt good about the excellent turnout. But can you imagine his surprise when God told him he had too many men?

God kept cutting the number down until Gideon had only 300 men left. That was all he would need. God would take care of the rest.

The 300 men collected jars and trumpets and then advanced on the Midianites. Each jar had a lighted torch inside.

As they approached the Midianite camp they held their jars and trumpets ready. On the signal they all smashed their lighted jars against the ground and blew their trumpets.

The Midianites panicked and began running in different directions. In the confusion they started to fight each other. Finally they fled into the wilderness.

Just 300 soldiers were able to rout an entire army.

(Judges 6,7,8)

Can you say, "Shibboleth"?

This word is tricky. It doesn't look too hard to pronounce, but you had better be careful. Some men couldn't say the word correctly and lost their lives.

Long ago General Jephthah was fighting against the Ephraimites. He defeated his enemy and took control of the rivers and fords. The Ephraimite army split up and tried to come back across the rivers to their homeland. They came one, two, or half a dozen at a time.

The Ephraimites looked like everyone else. How could General Jephthah's men know if those crossing the river were friends or enemies?

They thought of a plan. The soldiers would ask each person to say *shibboleth* before he could cross the river. That shouldn't be too hard, except for one thing. The Ephraimites couldn't pronounce the *h*. They said, "Sibboleth."

As each person crossed the river he was stopped and asked to say, "Shibboleth." If he couldn't say the *h*, he was arrested immediately as an Ephraimite.

How do you say *shibboleth*?

(Judges 12:1-6)

Answer: SHIB-uh-leth

Why did grandpa die?

Have you ever been camping? It can be fun to put up a tent, gather firewood, and fish in a nearby stream. You can explore the forest, climb mountains, and roast marshmallows on an open fire.

Of course, that's the good side. Camping also has its problems. There's poison ivy to worry about and a billion mosquitoes aiming at your ankles and neck.

As much as you enjoy living in a tent, it can't last forever. Someday you have to put everything away and head home. Home is more comfortable, and storms aren't nearly as big a problem. At home you will be surrounded by your friends.

Grandfathers live in the world for years. But it is like living in a tent. A better home, a permanent home, a home surrounded by friends waits for them in heaven.

Camping can't last forever. Neither can life on earth. The day will come to fold up our tents and go to a heavenly home that will never go away.

God understands that. He watches over his people while they live here. But then the great time comes. It's time to pack up and go home. God reaches his arm out, and welcomes grandpa in the name of Jesus Christ. Then we are happy for grandpa, because he has reached the best place of all. (2 Corinthians 5:1-8)

Have you ever wondered why God allows things to happen that are wrong? Certainly if God wanted to, he could stop such things from happening. For instance, he could put a gigantic plastic bag over every bank each night to stop bank robberies. If a robber came, he would bounce off the bag and fall down. He wouldn't be able to see the bag, and he couldn't pass through it. In the morning God could just pick up the bags again.

But God doesn't do that. He wants to leave it up to us. Do we want to be good to each other, or do we want to rob and cheat each other? God hopes we will decide to be kind, helpful, and godly.

Sometimes people fail. That is why banks need locks and guards. Sometimes people win. Millions of us will never rob a bank, or seriously harm another person.

Giant plastic bags would be easy for God. However, he would rather have us decide to do what is right.

Why does God allow bank robberies?

Far-out Facts

Some sheep in Bible days had tails that weighed fifteen pounds.

One of the favorite medicines was goat's milk.

Children were expected to be able to read the Bible at the age of five. Many began at three. Other schooling did not start until six or seven.

People with flat noses could not be priests.
(Leviticus 21:18, King James Version)

A Jewish teacher was always a man.

Students who did not pay good attention could be beaten with a strap.

Pupils wrote the lessons on wax paper stretched across a wooden tablet.

Cain was the first child to be born.

The members of Solomon's palace ate 450 bushels of grain and 130 animals each day.
(1 Kings 4:22,23; Good News Bible)

There were many blind people around Jerusalem because of diseases, accidents, and poor medical care.

Nebuchadnezzar's walls of Babylon were so wide that two chariots could drive on them side by side. He built two walls around the city with a dry moat outside to protect Babylon from an enemy army.

oliath's armor
ay have weighed
0-to-150 pounds.

Hebrew children ate honey for candy.

Solomon probably wrote the most songs in the Bible—1,005.

Do you feel funny when you see a black cat? Do you think a broken mirror will bring seven years of bad luck? Do you feel spooky if you walk under a ladder?

Many people are superstitious. Some knock on wood for good luck. Others check the stars to see if this will be a lucky day.

King Nebuchadnezzar of Babylon was so superstitious he did silly things just to check his luck.

Before Nebuchadnezzar went into battle he would "read the liver." An animal was sacrificed to a false god, and then its liver was "read." The size and color of the liver told the king whether or not to attack.

He also might read arrows. Four or five arrows were rolled around in a quiver, and then tossed on the ground. If the arrows pointed in the wrong direction, he told his soldiers to go back to bed.

Watch out for

The king also hired magicians to read the stars. If a few stars were in the wrong position, Nebuchadnezzar told his men to hang up their spears.

Superstitions are a lot of nonsense, and yet many of us believe them. It makes far more sense to trust in God than foolish luck. Neither arrows, black cats, nor stars can manage our life, but God would like to. Only he controls tomorrow.

black cats?

The Word Doctor

The wise men came from afar.
They followed a gigantic

_____.

(Matthew 2:1-2)

Herod's wife was filled with dread,
So she cut off John the Baptist's

_____.

(Matthew 14:6-11)

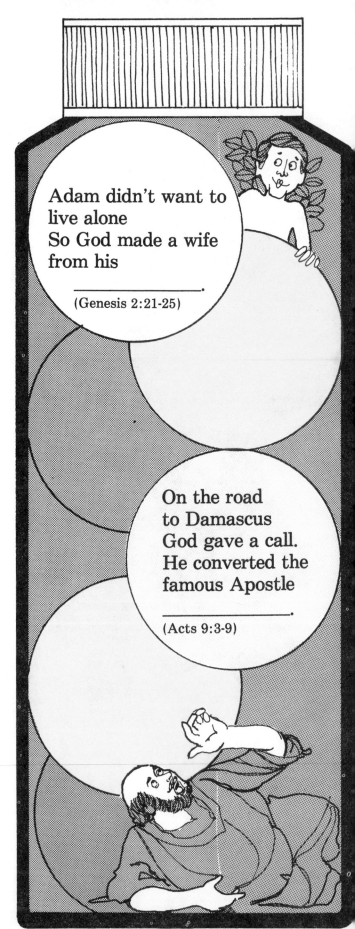

Adam didn't want to live alone
So God made a wife from his

_____.

(Genesis 2:21-25)

On the road to Damascus
God gave a call.
He converted the famous Apostle

_____.

(Acts 9:3-9)

These rhymes need help. What word would you prescribe to finish them?

Collecting animals
two by two
Noah soon had
a floating
_____.
(Genesis 7:13-16)

They refused to get
up and travel.
They built the huge
tower of
_____.
(Genesis 11:1-9)

Their enemies care-
fully plot and conspire
To throw the Hebrew
men in the
_____.
(Daniel 3:13-29)

Jesus had good news
he wanted to tell,
So he waited for the
woman at the
_____.
(John 4:6-42)

Answers: star, head, bone,
Paul, zoo, Babel, fire, well.

The Woman with the Scarlet Thread (Joshua 2)

Rahab is one of the most famous spies. She lived in Jericho and made a deal with the Israelite soldiers. The crafty lady hid Jewish spies in her home while they looked over the land.

In return for helping them, the spies promised to rescue her. She tied a scarlet thread from her window when the Israelite soldiers attacked. They saw the thread, and the Jews rescued Rahab and her family. The rest of the city was destroyed.

The Spies Who Were Ignored

(Numbers 13:17-33; 14:1-25)

Moses sent a dozen spies to check out the land of Canaan. They were to see if the people lived in tents or buildings or forts. Did their armies look strong? They were also to bring back samples of the food.

The spies spent forty days in the land and reported to Moses. Most of the spies were frightened by what they saw. "We seemed like grasshoppers. The people we saw there are of great size," they reported.

But Caleb disagreed. "We should go up and take the land," he said.

An argument raged among the people. Because of their fear, they didn't attack for almost forty years.

The Spy Who Stole (Joshua 7)

Achan was one of the soldiers Joshua sent to spy on the city of Ai. He reported back that the

It has always been dangerous to be a spy. If t were caught behind enemy lines, they could be killed immediately.

The Bible has a number of fascinating spy sto Here are a few. You find more.

Secret agents and spies

city would be easy to take.

But Achan ignored God's command to take no loot during the battle. He stole a beautiful robe, silver, and gold. Israel lost the battle. When the Israelites learned what Achan had done, they stoned him to death.

Down to Half a Beard
(2 Samuel 10)

The king of Ammon died. When King David heard about it, he felt sad. David decided to send some of his servants to see if they could help the new king.

When David's men arrived, someone told the new king of Ammon that these men were spies. He cut off half their beards and sent them home.

This was terribly embarrassing. David sent word to his servants to stay away until the other half of their beards grew back.

They Tried to Make a King (2 Samuel 15:10)

Absalom wanted to become king of Israel. But first, he had to remove his father, David.

He sent spies to all the tribes of Israel. They told the people to listen for the sound of a trumpet. When they heard it, everyone was to yell, "Absalom is king!"

The plot didn't work. Later Absalom was killed.

Sent to Trap Jesus
(Luke 20:20)

Christ's enemies sent spies to mix in the crowds that listened to Jesus. They were to pretend to be friendly. Their real job was to report everything he said.

Why do people pray?

Prayer is talking to God. Many times we have things we want to say to him. We have conversations with our parents for the same reason. In many ways talking to God is like talking to others.

This is just a short list of reasons why people pray.

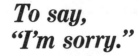

To say, "I'm sorry."

All of us have felt badly about something we have done. Maybe we took something that didn't belong to us. Possibly we lied. Once in a while we hurt someone. We tell others when we are sorry. Often we want God to know how we feel, too. When we tell God we are sorry, he always forgives us.

(1 John 1:9)

To say, "Thank you."

We have something we are especially pleased with, and we want to say so. Maybe it is a healthy body, good parents, a new bike. Just like we thank people who are nice to us, we often want to thank God.

(1 Thessalonians 5:18)

To ask for things.

You might need something very badly. Maybe it is food or clothing. Possibly a

These are just a few examples.   *How many more reasons*

To ask for wisdom.

It can be difficult to make decisions. Should we go here or there? Is this friend good for me or not? Should I volunteer to play in the band?

Both children and adults could use help in making decisions. We often take these things to God and ask him to show us which way is best.

(James 1:5)

To calm down.

Once in a while we become caught up in doing too many things. We have to be here, and do this, and get that ready. It is possible to become so busy we think we can't handle everything.

At times like this it helps to get alone and talk to God. Sometimes we just sit quietly. Our mind stops racing and our body becomes calm. After "visiting" with God, we often feel better and can deal with life a little easier.

(Psalms 46:1; Isaiah 30:15)

riend or relative is in he hospital, and you vant them to get well. The Bible tells us to xplain what we want o God. He is happy o listen to the millions f requests he gets very day.

God might give you xactly what you want. He also could say no. Either way, he wants to ear from his children.

(John 14:14; Matthew 6:5-15)

o you think people have for praying?

35

How do people pray?

Most people we know close their eyes when they pray. However, others have prayed in almost every position you can imagine. Here are a few things people have done while praying.

A tax collector beat on his chest like a drum (Luke 18:13).

Samuel's mother, Hannah, prayed by moving her lips but without talking out loud. A priest saw her and thought she was drunk (1 Samuel 1:12,13)

Many people stood up to pray (Matthew 6:5)

Peter found a quiet place on his flat roof (Acts 10:9).

Solomon prayed with his spread hands pointing toward heaven (1 Kings 8:22)

Elijah prayed in a sitting position with his face between his knees (1 Kings 18:42).

Some prayed facing the temple in Jerusalem (1 Kings 8:38).

Job prayed by falling flat on the ground (Job 1:20).

Many people have doubted either God, the Bible, prayer, or something else. It isn't wrong to doubt. Sometimes doubt can lead to a strong faith.

Doubt is at its best if it makes you ask questions. Will you search to find the right answer? Will you ask parents, ministers, friends until you are satisfied? Will you read the Bible in hope of finding information? Then doubt is good, healthy, even helpful.

Some people like to doubt. They want to keep their doubts and don't look for answers. This type of doubt is harmful and will get you no place.

The most famous doubter in the Bible is the Apostle Thomas. He said he would not believe Jesus had come back from the dead unless he could touch him.

Jesus wasn't mad at Thomas for doubting. He showed his wounded hands and feet to the apostle. Thomas's doubts paid off, because he got the answer.

(John 20:24-28)

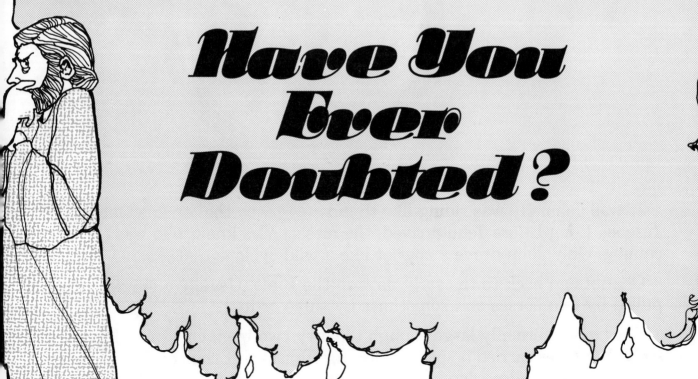

Have You Ever Doubted?

Jehu, The Hot Rod

The chariot came tearing down the road. Dust flew up in large brown clouds behind him. Who was the rider racing his two-horse chariot with the iron-rimmed wheels?

It was Jehu. He was riding like thunder to reach the terrible Queen Jezebel. Long before Jehu arrived, the messengers knew who was coming. Only Jehu drove a chariot like a wild cyclone (2 Kings 9:20).

Chariots go back to the early days in the Bible. Usually a chariot was pulled by two horses and sometimes by three or four.

They were normally large enough to carry two men. One man drove while the other carried a spear, ready for fighting. If the chariot was big enough, it could also carry a soldier with a shield. Even a fourth man could be packed in.

Imagine how foot soldiers felt when dozens of chariots charged them.

At times the Hebrews faced such difficult odds because they did not have chariots. But God often rescued them. When the Egyptians tried to stop the Jews, Egypt's 600 chariots became stuck in the mud of the Red Sea.
(Exodus 14-15)

Joshua defeated Jabin's army by burning their chariots.
(Joshua 11:9)

Later King David captured a thousand chariots and seven thousand charioteers. He began to build an army of chariots. His son, Solomon, developed a first-class chariot army—so large he built chariot cities to hold these troops and protect Israel's borders.
(2 Samuel 8:4; 1 Kings 9:19)

DETECTIVE CLUEDO

Case No. 17041

Crime: Running away

See how few clues you need to find the missing person.

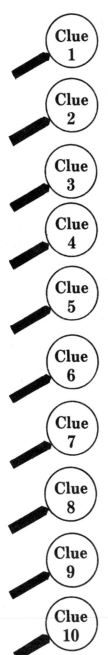

Clue 1   Asked to do something

Clue 2   Didn't like the job

Clue 3   Went to Joppa

Clue 4   Liked the sea better

Clue 5   Caught ship to Tarshish

Clue 6   Storm almost wrecked his ship

Clue 7   Cargo thrown over

Clue 8   Suspect thrown over

Clue 9   Swallowed by fish

Clue 10   Told Nineveh it would be destroyed

Answer: *Jonah* (Book of Jonah)

6-10 clues—You are a GRAND
               DETECTIVE.
1-5 clues—You are a SUPER DETECTIVE.

Case No. 17042

Crime: Missing child

*See how few clues you need
to find the missing child.*

DETECTIVE CLUEDO

 Clue 1

 Clue 2

 Clue 3

 Clue 4

 Clue 5

 Clue 6

 Clue 7

 Clue 8

 Clue 9

Clue 10

Child is Hebrew

Child was to be killed

Mother protected child

Special bed was made

Sister watched the bed

Bed was placed in water

Maidens found baby

They told Pharaoh's daughter

Pharaoh's daughter adopts child

Real mother asked to take care of child

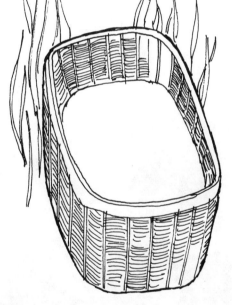

Answer: *Moses* (Exodus 2:1-10)

6-10 clues—You are a GRAND
DETECTIVE.
1-5 clues—You are a SUPER DETECTIVE.

41

Do you like contests?

It's fun to win. No doubt about it. If you have ever won at anything, you know how Elijah must have felt one day on Mount Carmel.

The contest was important. People from all over Israel had gathered to find out who was the real God. Was it the god of Baal or the Lord God?

Elijah was outnumbered. He was the only prophet for God. There were 450 prophets of Baal against him.

Quickly, the prophets of Baal cut up their meat sacrifice and placed it on the wood. All Baal had to do was send down fire. If he burned up the sacrifice, he must be God.

The prophets started praying. Nothing happened. They began to dance. Nothing happened. They kept it up from morning until noon. Nothing happened.

While all this noise went on, Elijah was laughing. Then he started making fun of the prophets.

"Louder!" he yelled. "Maybe your god is talking to somebody."

"Louder!" he bellowed. "Maybe your god is on vacation."

"Louder!" he roared. "Maybe your god is taking a nap."

Each time Elijah laughed harder, and the prophets of Baal wailed louder. But nothing happened.

All afternoon the prophets shouted. They cut themselves with knives and swords as was their custom. They pleaded. But nothing happened.

When evening started to fall, Elijah stopped laughing and called everyone to come close.

He built an altar of twelve stones. Wood was placed on it. Then he dug a ditch around the altar. A meat sacrifice was placed on the altar.

He called for four jars of water and poured them on the sacrifice. Then he called for four more. And just to make sure the altar was wet, he called for four more. The ditch and altar were drowned in water.

Calmly Elijah asked God to show himself.

Bang! Fire flashed out of heaven. It burned up the meat, the wood, the stones, and dried all the water out of the ditch.

God had won the contest!

(1 Kings 18:18-39)

Did you know?

Olives and grapes were the fruit most often eaten.

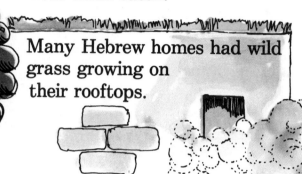

Many Hebrew homes had wild grass growing on their rooftops.

Anyone who owed money could be arrested and jailed until he paid every penny.

Hebrew homes had no chimneys. Smoke had to escape out the windows.

Wrestling was a favorite sport among Hebrew youth.

Hebrew families had board games something like our Monopoly or Scrabble.

The winners of athletic contests were
often given a crown made of leaves.

In Roman games men often
had to wrestle animals.

Before a youth could
compete in a sport at the
Greek stadiums, he had
to promise he had
trained for at least ten
months.

If your brother died, you
were expected to marry
his wife.

45

Why would anyone steal buttons?

Most children don't need them. The round little things don't taste very good, either. Why would anyone steal a package of buttons?

Andy had his own reasons.

To begin with, it looked so easy. They just sat on the open shelf. Andy knew his lightning hand could snatch one in a split second.

Besides, many of Andy's friends claimed that they had stolen things from the store. Andy had seen some of them. A pocket knife. A box of caps. Nothing really big.

Andy didn't want his friends to think he was a scaredy-cat. He had planned to show the buttons to his friends, and then throw them down the sewer. Instead, he was sitting in the manager's office, waiting for his mother to come.

Like everyone else, Andy had been tempted or tested. It might have helped if he had known what the Bible says about temptation:

Everyone thinks about doing something bad. Maybe it isn't stealing buttons. It might be lying, hating, fighting. All of us are tempted to do something.

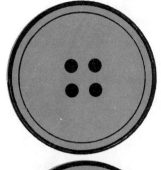

Our thoughts and actions are not strange or weird. We are like everyone else.

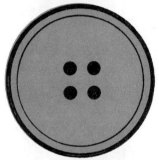

God is willing to help us stay away from doing wrong. When we want to lie, we ask God to help us resist it.

All of us could say no to doing something bad. We can get away from it, because God is willing to help us resist temptation.

When we are about to do something wrong, it often helps to read 1 Corinthians 10:13:

But remember this—the wrong desires that come into your life aren't anything new and different. Many others have faced exactly the same problems before you. And no temptation is irresistible. You can trust God to keep the temptation from becoming so strong that you can't stand up against it, for He has promised this and will do what He says. He will show you how to escape temptation's power so that you can bear up patiently against it.

(The Living Bible)   47

Have you ever seen food come from heaven like rain? Could you strike a rock and make water come out? All of this is possible when God moves in nature. These are just a few of the stories found in the Bible.

The Sundial Went Backward
(2 Kings 20, King James Version)

A shadow on a sundial goes forward as the sun moves. They can't go backward. The sun would have to back up, like a car, to make a shadow move that way. It can't. But it did.

The prophet Isaiah told King Hezekiah that his health would get better. Hezekiah didn't believe him and asked for a sign from God.

He got one. God moved the shadow on the sundial backward ten points. It can't. But it did.

Food from Heaven
(Exodus 16)

When the nation of Israel traveled in the wilderness, they had a terrible time getting enough food—until God took over.

One morning they woke up to find small flakes covering the ground. The people picked up the tiny pieces, made them into cakes, and fed each person. The next day more food was there. They called it manna.

The Stick Became a Snake   (Exodus 7:6-13)

Moses and Aaron had a special message from God for the pharaoh of Egypt. But how

Nature did

more funny things

would the pharaoh know they came from God?

God had a plan. When Moses and Aaron faced the pharaoh, Aaron threw his stick on the floor. Immediately it turned into a living snake.

The Raven Food Service
(1 Kings 17)

Elijah was a good prophet, but King Ahab hated him. God told his prophet to go and hide before he got hurt. Elijah went to a brook near the Jordan River.

While he was hiding, God took care of him. He sent black ravens to carry food. Each morning the birds brought bread and meat to the prophet.

The Rock with a Faucet
(Exodus 17:1-7)

There wasn't enough water in the wilderness. God told Moses how to get some. All they had to do was strike a certain rock, and water would pour out.

Moses struck the rock twice with a stick. Immediately water poured out as if someone had opened a faucet full blast.

Walking on Water
(Mark 6:45-52)

Skiing on water can be hard. Walking on it is impossible. We are heavier than water, so it simply won't work. But, somehow Jesus walked on water.

Can you imagine how surprised the disciples must have been? About 3:00 A.M. they saw someone walking past their boat. When he got closer, they discovered it was Jesus Christ.

Old And NEW

Don't look yet!

This is a time quiz. To do it get either:
1. Someone to count to 1,000, 2,000, or 10,000
2. Get a time buzzer
3. Race against a friend

How fast can you decide whether these people are mentioned in the Old Testament or the New Testament? Just write *O* or *N* on a paper that has been numbered from 1 to 30.

Set? Go!

Deduct two points for each one wrong.

1. Mary
2. Moses
3. Paul
4. Philemon
5. Eunice
6. Adam
7. Caiaphas
8. Samson
9. Pilate
10. Barnabas

11. Ezekiel
12. Jonah
13. Mark
14. Naomi
15. Herod
16. Daniel
17. Lois
18. Ruth
19. Samuel
20. John

21. Apollos
22. Sarah
23. Rahab
24. Peter
25. Nicodemus
26. David
27. Noah
28. Joshua
29. Jeremiah
30. Timothy

Answers: 1—N 2—O 3—N 4—N 5—N 6—O 7—N 8—O 9—N 10—N 11—O 12—O 13—N 14—O 15—N 16—O 17—N 18—O 19—O 20—N 21—N 22—O 23—O 24—N 25—N 26—O 27—O 28—O 29—O 30—N

50

Many famous people in the Bible had famous partners.

Your job is to be a matchmaker. How many people can you put with the correct partner? Number your paper from 1-10 and put the correct letters beside the numbers.

MATCHMAKER

1. Abraham	a. Mary
2. Samson	b. Bathsheba
3. David	c. Jacob
4. Joseph	d. Rebekah
5. Jezebel	e. Delilah
6. Rachel	f. Sarah
7. Isaac	g. Priscilla
8. Aquila	h. Boaz
9. Adam	i. Eve
10. Ruth	j. Ahab

If you got 1-3 correct, you are a MATCHMAKER.

If you got 4-7 correct, you are a GOOD MATCHMAKER.

If you got 8-10 correct, you are a SUPER MATCHMAKER.

Answers: 1—f 2—e 3—b 4—a 5—j 6—c 7—d 8—g 9—i 10—h

51

Rings are fun. Some people wear them to show what school they graduated from. Others wear them because of their special beauty. In the Bible, people wore rings for fascinating reasons.

As an ornament

Rebekah, Isaac's beautiful bride, wore a ring in her nose.

(Genesis 24:47)

As a signature

A king's ring was used to place his special seal in wax on letters or documents.

(Esther 3:12)

As a reward

The king of Persia gave a ring to Mordecai to show his favor.

(Esther 8:2)

Why wear rings?

For authority

Joseph was given a special ring to prove he represented the pharaoh.

(Genesis 41:42)

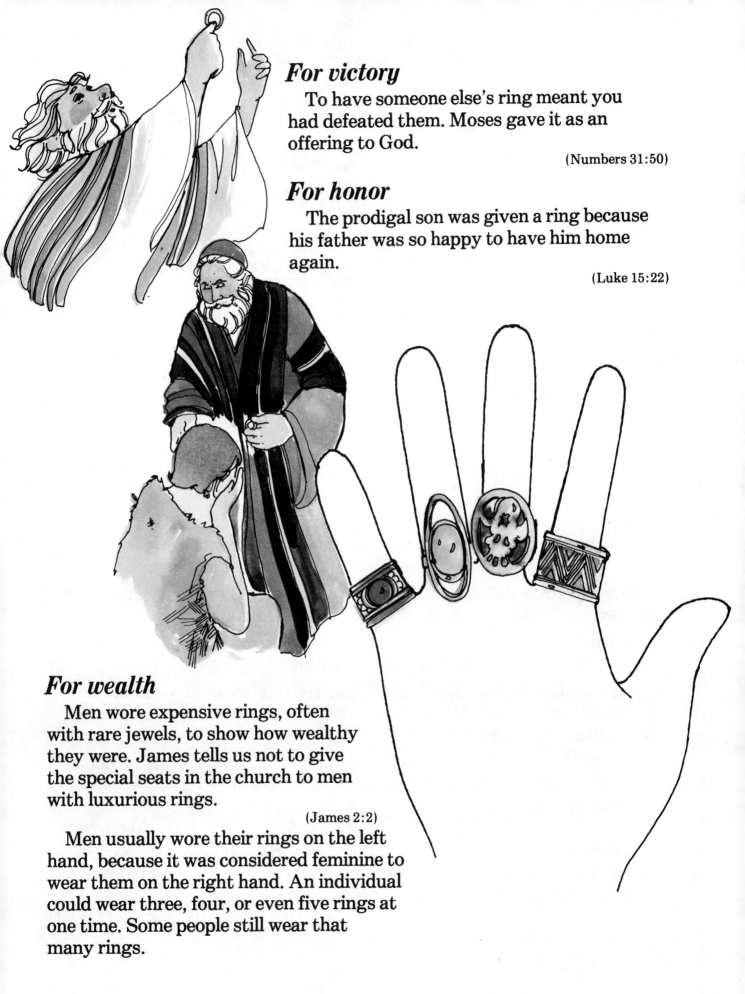

For victory

To have someone else's ring meant you had defeated them. Moses gave it as an offering to God.

(Numbers 31:50)

For honor

The prodigal son was given a ring because his father was so happy to have him home again.

(Luke 15:22)

For wealth

Men wore expensive rings, often with rare jewels, to show how wealthy they were. James tells us not to give the special seats in the church to men with luxurious rings.

(James 2:2)

Men usually wore their rings on the left hand, because it was considered feminine to wear them on the right hand. An individual could wear three, four, or even five rings at one time. Some people still wear that many rings.

The Witch of Endor

Many people in the Bible could be described as witches. Magicians and sorcerers lived in both large cities and small towns. They could make mysterious things happen, which no one could explain.

One woman is definitely called a witch. She lived at Endor and claimed she could talk to the dead.

When Saul, the king of Israel, saw the Philistine armies gathered against him, he was terrified. He needed help.

Saul went to see the Witch of Endor. He wanted to know if she could contact Samuel. If Saul could talk to his dead friend, he was sure he could get some good advice.

The Witch of Endor did something that we don't understand. Soon she saw an old man dressed in a robe. The spirit spoke and discussed the war with Saul.

(1 Samuel 28)

Whatever actually happened, this was a serious mistake for Saul. One of the reasons that Saul died was because he had contacted the Witch of Endor.

(1 Chronicles 10:13,14)

A STRANGE CURSE

After Joshua destroyed the famous city of Jericho, he placed a curse on it. He promised that if anyone ever rebuilt Jericho as a fortified city, that man's oldest and youngest sons would die.

For hundreds of years people believed this curse, and no one dared rebuild the fortified walls of Jericho. Then a few began to laugh at it.

Finally Hiel, a Bethelite, decided to take action. No one could tell him what to do. Hiel laid the foundation. His son, Abiram, died. Hiel probably claimed it was just a freak accident.

He went on with the building. When he put up the city gate, his youngest son, Segub, died.

Joshua's strange curse had been fulfilled.

(Joshua 6:26; 1 Kings 16:34)

Adam

There was a man, all alone,
Had no family, wife, or home.
One day he burst with great pride,
He found a wife right by his side.
(Genesis 2:20-23)

What do angels do?

Angels must be very busy. One of their jobs is to protect Christians. We have angels who watch over us (Psalm 91:11; Hebrews 1:14).

This isn't their only job. They probably do many things we have never known. In the New Testament angels are often seen making special announcements and protecting individuals.

An angel anounced the birth of both John the Baptist and Jesus.

(Luke 1:11-20; 2:8-14)

Mary and Joseph were warned by an angel to flee to Egypt because their lives were in danger.

(Matthew 2:13)

Angels helped Jesus after Satan tempted him.

(Luke 22:43)

The stone in front of Jesus'
tomb was rolled away by angels.
(Matthew 28:2,3)

An angel helped Peter escape
from prison.
(Acts 12:7-10)

Philip was told by an angel to
leave Jerusalem and travel to the
Gaza Desert.
(Acts 8:26)

Some who thought they had
entertained people in their homes
had really opened their homes
to angels.
(Hebrews 13:2)

We probably can't know all
that angels have done in our
lives. But someday maybe
we will.

Job's Sea Monster

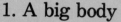

Thousands of years ago Job described an enormous sea animal. Was it a real monster or just pretend? You be the judge. Take a piece of paper and draw it using Job's description. Make it a monster for both land and sea. Job called it a leviathan. (Job 41)

1. A big body
2. Large and graceful limbs
3. Fearsome teeth
4. A back that looks like rows of shields, tightly sealed together
5. Eyes that glow like sparks
6. Fire that leaps from its mouth
7. Smoke that flows from its nose
8. A chest as hard as rock
9. A strong neck that strikes terror
10. It laughs at javelins and spears.
11. A belly covered with scales
12. Its motion makes water boil.
13. It churns the depths.
14. It is king of all it sees.

He once was governor of the land.
On the problem of Jesus he took no stand.
With great show he washed his hands
And said, "I find no fault in this man."

(Matthew 27:15-26)

Pilate

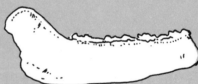

Don't think too hard,
No need to groan.
Who killed those men
With an old jawbone?

(Judges 15:14-16)

Samson

Words Words Words

Many words go over our heads. We hear them often, but don't know what they mean. If we learn a few, it might be a big help.

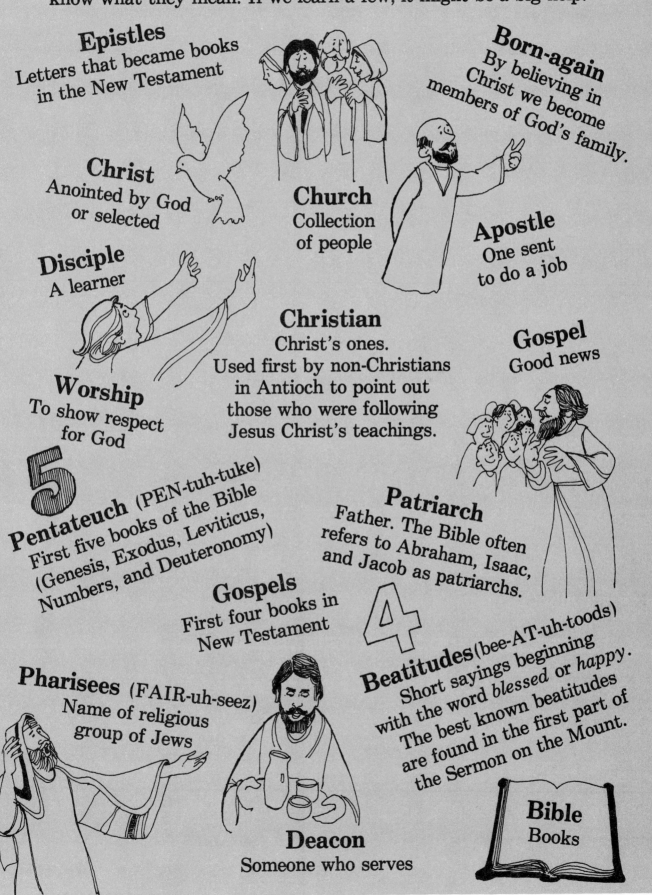

Epistles
Letters that became books in the New Testament

Born-again
By believing in Christ we become members of God's family.

Christ
Anointed by God or selected

Church
Collection of people

Apostle
One sent to do a job

Disciple
A learner

Christian
Christ's ones. Used first by non-Christians in Antioch to point out those who were following Jesus Christ's teachings.

Gospel
Good news

Worship
To show respect for God

Pentateuch (PEN-tuh-tuke)
First five books of the Bible (Genesis, Exodus, Leviticus, Numbers, and Deuteronomy)

Patriarch
Father. The Bible often refers to Abraham, Isaac, and Jacob as patriarchs.

Gospels
First four books in New Testament

Beatitudes (bee-AT-uh-toods)
Short sayings beginning with the word *blessed* or *happy*. The best known beatitudes are found in the first part of the Sermon on the Mount.

Pharisees (FAIR-uh-seez)
Name of religious group of Jews

Bible
Books

Deacon
Someone who serves

Who wants to eat wood bark three time

Probably no one. But in Bible times wood bark, animal brains, and liver were used as medicines. If you had an unusual sickness, many different remedies were tried. Almost anything was added to the list.

Even the treatment for ordinary ailments was strange. Pretend you are sick. Here's what might have happened to you.

Do you have a fever?

The doctor probably would have put little worms called leeches on your skin. Leeches would suck out your blood. When you lost enough blood, you were supposed to get well. If you lost too much blood, you would probably die.

Do you need an operation?

Most of the time, the doctor couldn't put you to sleep. Some drugs might deaden the pain, but usually you would be awake for at least part of the operation —until you fainted.

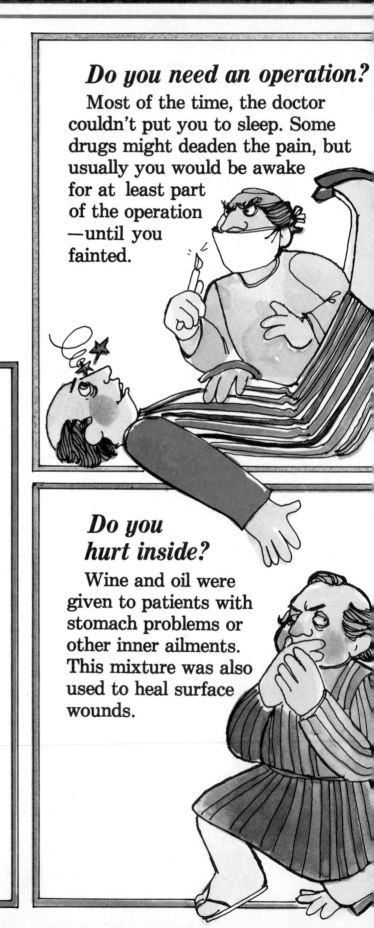

Do you hurt inside?

Wine and oil were given to patients with stomach problems or other inner ailments. This mixture was also used to heal surface wounds.

a day?

Do you need false teeth?

First the old ones must be pulled. This was often painful and much bleeding could follow.

New teeth would be made from wood, gold, or silver. Sometimes the false teeth didn't fit very well.

Do you have boils?

Scrape your neck with a piece of broken pottery. Maybe you should apply wet ashes or mud. (Job 2:8)

Do you have gangrene?

If you got this in your toes, fingers, arms, or legs, you were always in for a bad time. Doctors would try to cut off your limb. But few patients lived. If the gangrene didn't kill you, the operation was almost sure to.

Do you often have headaches or strange sicknesses?

You could find a doctor to operate on your skull. With little to stop the pain, he would chisel a piece of the bone out of your head. If the headaches didn't go away, he would chisel out another piece. The operations were probably worse than the headaches.

How do you know a door is real? You can see a door, feel the wood, and hear it slam. If you don't see the door and run into it, you could hurt your head.

You know a door is real because you can see, hear, and feel it.

You can hear what God has done. The Bible is filled with stories of how he performed miracles and guided people. We also hear stories of how he helps people today.

You can experience God's power.

Is God real like a door?

God is just as real as a door. Even though you cannot see him and feel him, you can see what God has done. Animals, flowers, snowflakes, and eyes all have a design to them. They are the work of the Great Creator.

After you pray about something, you often see what he does. You know God works.

We can see, hear, and experience. Then we have to choose if we want to believe. If you believe, God is just as real as a door.

Why doesn't God stop hunger?

God can't be happy about starving people. He does not like to see children whose bones are showing through their skin. God doesn't want to see people digging in garbage piles looking for food.

Suppose God wanted to do something about hunger. So he told the Christians to feed the hungry. But we did not want to help because we were too busy doing other things.

We say, "Why doesn't God do something?" Maybe God is saying, "Why don't the Christians do something?"

We could be God's way to stop hunger.

In the Bible it says, *"Suppose a brother or sister is without clothes and daily food. If one of you says to him, 'Go, I wish you well; keep warm and well fed,' but does nothing about his physical needs, what good is it?"*

(James 2:15,16)

Those Amazing Kings

This is what the Bible calls King Manasseh. He was only twelve when he took the throne. From the beginning Manasseh did almost every evil thing he could think of.

He tried to get information by asking witches. Large statues were built to false gods and idols. Manasseh attempted to talk to the dead.

One idol was built with metal hands. The hands were heated red hot, and children were sacrificed in the hands. Manasseh may have put his own child in those hands.

The Bible says Jerusalem was filled with blood from one end to the other during his time. After many years of evil Manasseh repented and turned to God.

The King Who Became Like an Animal (Daniel 4:28-37)

This is no fairy tale. Babylon had a king named Nebuchadnezzar. He built the Hanging Gardens of Babylon, one of the wonders of the world.

Nebuchadnezzar became extremely proud of all he had done. One day he was bragging, and God spoke to the king and told him he would be like an animal.

Immediately Nebuchadnezzar was driven away from the people and began to eat grass in the field like an ox. At night he slept on the ground. His hair grew like the feathers of an eagle and his nails like the claws of a bird.

Finally Nebuchadnezzar raised his eyes to heaven, and his sanity was restored. He had learned a lesson about giving credit to God.

Israel's army moved into Canaan and started capturing land. During this time they fought the mean king Adoni-Bezek (uh-DOH-ni BEE-zek), king of Bezek.

When the soldiers caught him, they cut off his thumbs and big toes. Without them, he could no longer throw a spear or run as well.

That sounds cruel, but it didn't surprise King Adoni-Bezek. He told them he had cut the thumbs and toes off seventy other kings.

He Cut Off Thumbs and Toes

(Judges 1:1-7)

The Kindness of King David

(2 Samuel 4:4; 19:24-30)

When Saul and Jonathan were killed, Jonathan left a five-year-old son. He had been in the care of a nurse. When the slaughter began, she escaped with the boy. As the nurse ran she tripped, and the boy broke both ankles. He was never able to walk again.

The boy's name was Mephibosheth (muh-FIB-uh-sheth).

They found a place to hide him, and there he grew up. Later he married, but he was always crippled.

When King David defeated his enemies, he went looking for the boy who was King Saul's grandson. Mephibosheth thought the king was going to kill him. Instead David gave the crippled man land that others could farm. He then moved him to Jerusalem and invited him to eat regularly at the palace.

Kings weren't always mean or rough.

He Pretended to Be Crazy

SCRATCH
SCRATCH

(1 Samuel 21:10-15)

Sometimes David had to think fast to keep himself out of trouble. King Saul was jealous and didn't want David to become king.

During one of these dangerous times David was visiting Achish, king of Gath. While there, some men recognized him and wondered if they should arrest him.

When David heard this, he started to pretend. He began scratching at the door like a puppy. Then he let spit run down his beard. When the people saw what he was doing, they decided he was crazy and let him go.

King David must have been a terrific actor.

Which are real?

The Old Testament has ten famous and important commandments. Can you pick out the real ones?

1. You shall not lie.
2. You shall not borrow.
3. You shall not fight.
4. You shall not steal.
5. You shall not argue.
6. You shall not kill.
7. You shall not worship idols.
8. You shall not be slothful.
9. You shall not envy.
10. You shall not commit adultery.

11. You shall not disobey the police.
12. You shall keep the Sabbath.
13. You shall honor your parents.
14. You shall not stay up late.
15. You shall not use God's name in vain.
16. You shall worship no other God.

The real commandments are numbers 1, 4, 6, 7, 9, 10, 12, 13, 15, 16 (Exodus 20:2-17).

EMPLOYMENT OFFICE

The biblical people in column A have come to your office looking for a job. You have to match them with the job that best describes the work they do. The match is somewhere in column B. Number your paper from 1-20 and put the right letter beside the number.

Seeking Employment
Column A

1. Tanner
2. Muleteer
3. Caravan chief
4. Herald
5. Publican
6. Scribe
7. Spy
8. Census taker
9. Barber
10. Mason
11. Apothecary
12. Peddler
13. Pawnbroker
14. King
15. Surveyor
16. Ferryman
17. Chorister
18. Harness maker
19. Prophet
20. Rabbi

Jobs Available
Column B

a. Count people
b. Secretary
c. Mule driver
d. Pharmacist
e. Teacher
f. Leather work
g. Build stonework
h. Predict future
i. Lead travelers
j. Measure land
k. Guide boats
l. Sing
m. Make royal announcements
n. Make harnesses
o. Tax collector
p. Rule over a group of people
q. Loan money
r. Sell goods
s. Shave beards
t. Collect secrets

1-5 ☆   6-10 ☆☆   11-15 ☆☆☆   16-20 ☆☆☆☆

Answers: 1—f 2—c 3—i 4—m 5—o 6—b 7—t 8—a 9—s 10—g 11—d 12—r 13—q 14—p 15—j 16—k 17—l 18—n 19—h 20—e

We remember Adolph Hitler as a man who hated Jews. During World War II he had about 6 million Jews killed. Other men have tried to eliminate the Jews.

One was Haman, a man in Persia. He ended up with a big surprise.

Because Haman was prime minister, he believed every man should bow down to him. But one man, a Jew named Mordecai, refused. He believed a person should bow only before God.

Haman became furious. He convinced the king that all the Jews in Persia should be executed. The date was set for February 28. Each person who

We don't know how tall King Og was. He was the king of over sixty cities in the land of Bashan.

King Og was defeated by Israelites. When they captured his bed, they decided to keep it. The bed was made of iron, and they placed it in a museum.

The gigantic

Hitler Haman

killed a Jew could claim that Jew's property.

Queen Esther heard about the terrible plan. She was a Jewish orphan who had been raised by Mordecai. She admitted to the king that she was Jewish and convinced him to save her people.

Haman was hanged on the special, seventy-five foot gallows he had built for Mordecai.

(Book of Esther, The Living Bible)

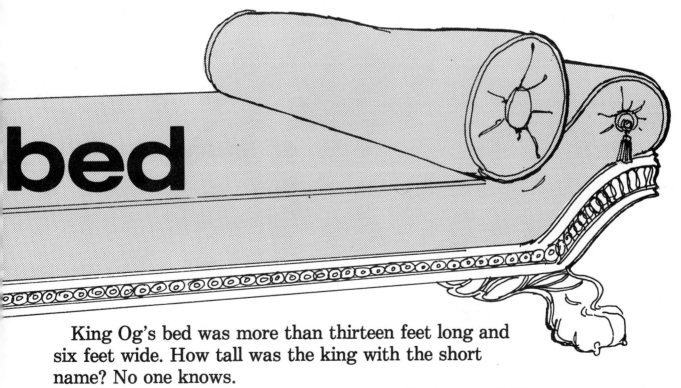

bed

King Og's bed was more than thirteen feet long and six feet wide. How tall was the king with the short name? No one knows.

(Deuteronomy 3:11)

Did you know?

Many farmers lived in town and went out to the country daily to work.

Playing marbles goes back at least 3,500 years.

The first operation in the Bible was for Adam's rib.

Cornelius was the first gentile to become a Christian.

The first miracle by Jesus was probably the changing of water into wine at Cana.

Lydia was probably the first person in Europe to become a Christian.

70

Saul was Israel's first king.

When there was a death in the family, the men sometimes shaved their head bald.

Children read aloud in school, probably all at once.

Lot's wife is the only person to turn to salt.

A jot is the smallest letter in the Hebrew alphabet.

Is God married?

That's a smart question. Most of the people we see are married. Does God have a wife?

There are a few reasons to believe God is single. After you read them, you make up your own mind.

First, the Bible does not say God has a wife. If it said he did, the problem would be solved.

Second, God is a person but not a man. Even though we call him Father he is not like men on earth.

Third, he doesn't need a wife to have children. God can create by just talking. If he wanted to, he could make them out of leaves, twigs, bottle caps, or out of nothing.

Fourth, marriage is for human beings. Angels do not marry. People do not get married in heaven.

It doesn't sound like God has a wife. What do you think?

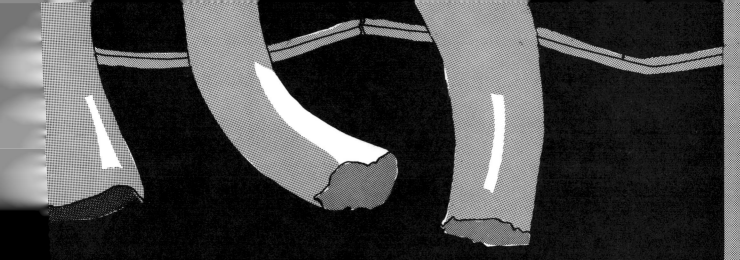

How could Jesus be resurrected?

Talk about great news! Jesus Christ has overcome death. He spent three days and nights in a tomb, dead, and then came back to life.

Death could not hold the Son of God. What does that mean to us?

Imagine that everyone was in a jail with iron bars. One day Jesus grabbed two bars and tore them off. Then, he walked outside the jail. Because Jesus did it, the rest of the people could walk out by using the opening Jesus made.

Death is like that jail. Jesus opened up death and walked out. That was his resurrection. Today, all of us can overcome death by believing in Jesus Christ. We will die but immediately we will live again.

But, how could Jesus be resurrected? He couldn't be, except by a miracle.

If God wanted to turn coconuts into stars, he could do it. If he wanted a stick to walk, he could even make it run.

A resurrection is no problem to God. Jesus was really dead. But God decided to perform a miracle. Now, Christ is alive forever.

Don't start yet!

ONE MINUTE MATCH

Number your paper from 1-10. You have one minute to match the Bible character and famous object in their life.

If you get 1-3 correct, you are a BEGINNER; 4-7 makes you a GOOD BEGINNER; 8-10 makes you a WINNER.

Person

1. David
2. Samson
3. Judas
4. Gideon
5. Peter
6. Jonah
7. Moses
8. Noah
9. Mary
10. Joseph

Objects

a. coat of colors
b. a fish
c. sling
d. burning bush
e. ark
f. jawbone
g. treasurer's bag
h. expensive perfume
i. fleece of wool
j. sheet with animals on it, descending from heaven

Answers: 1.c 2.f 3.g 4.i 5.j 6.b 7.d 8.e 9.h 10.a

ONE MINUTE MATCH

Don't start yet! Number your paper from 1-12. Now get a clock and time yourself. You have one minute to match the Bible characters and their jobs. *Some jobs will be used more than once.*

Person

1. Zacchaeus
2. Peter
3. Paul
4. Cornelius
5. Onesimus
6. Matthew
7. Lydia
8. David
9. Simon
10. Luke
11. Bartimaeus
12. Joseph

Job

a. Beggar
b. Tanner
c. Tax collector
d. Shepherd
e. Doctor
f. Fisherman
g. Carpenter
h. Slave
i. Tentmaker
j. Sold purple
k. Soldier

Answers: 1.c 2.f 3.i 4.k 5.h 6.c 7.j 8.d 9.b 10.e 11.a 12.g

Christ was often a friend to people who had many enemies. When almost no one liked them, Jesus would still show them he cared.

Look at some of the people Jesus became close to:

Simon the Leper

Leprosy was a terrible disease during the time of Christ. There were several types of leprosy. The most famous kind would make fingers, toes, and noses fall off. Often it could kill.

Most people stayed away from lepers. They were both sick and lonely.

Christ found lepers and became their friend.

He wasn't afraid to touch them (Luke 5:12,13).

A Samaritan Woman

Samaritans were from a different national background so many people disliked them. Their families were part Jewish and part gentile. Others made fun of them and called them names as we often do today.

Jesus knew it was wrong to tease and hate people because they were different. He decided to be their friend. Christ was called names for being nice to Samaritans (John 8:48). He didn't let it stop him (John 4:1-42).

Who were Jesus' friends? ?⦿

Zacchaeus, the tax collector

This man had a tough job. He had to collect taxes and give them to the government. Taxes were high. Many people thought Zacchaeus cheated them and charged too much. Most people hated him.

Zacchaeus climbed up in a tree to see Jesus walk past. But Jesus saw the short man and told him to come down. Christ invited himself to the tax collector's house for dinner (Luke 19:1-9). He asked another tax collector, Matthew Levi, to become a disciple (Mark 2:14).

Roman soldiers

Most Jews wanted the Roman soldiers to get out of Israel. People don't like having soldiers from another country in their streets.

Sometimes Roman soldiers were cruel and mean. At other times they were kind and even helpful.

Instead of fighting them, Christ tried to be their friend.

A Roman soldier's son became sick and could not walk. Christ showed his kindness by healing the boy (Matthew 8:5-13).

Children

Some people think children are not very important. They don't want them around. They seem to think children are worthless until they become adults.

Jesus knew each child was very valuable. He loved children, spent time with them, held them on his lap.

When some people objected and said to send the children away, Christ said to bring them near. He enjoyed

having young people around (Matthew 19:13-15).

Fishermen

Many of the men who lived around the Sea of Galilee worked as fishermen. They didn't own expensive homes or wear special clothes. They worked every day and were happy if they could keep their children fed.

Christ was also a working man. He made an extra effort to be their friend. Jesus asked some fishermen to be his followers (Matthew 4:18).

There are more people whom Jesus made his friends. Look for them in the Bible.

This is one way for a Christian to be like Christ. We all know someone who is lonely, picked on, maybe different. We can go to that person and be his special friend. This is what Jesus did often.

How did women get lovely?

Women like to look nice. Even in Bible times they wore makeup and worked hard to keep their hair in place. They had mirrors to make sure their appearance was just right.

Many women spent hours fixing their hair. They went to all the trouble of putting their hair in curlers. If they wanted to add color, a woman could dye her hair, sprinkle gold-colored dust on it, or wear a wig. A fancy hairdo was sometimes topped off with a fancy hairpin.

Special face powders and eye rouge were chosen to give a woman an attractive look. Tweezers have been found, so we know women plucked their eyebrows and painted them. Girls often had their own cosmetic boxes.

If a lady wanted a tan all year round, she rubbed oil on her body. This not only gave her a healthy look but also a pleasant smell.

Baths were a little harder to get in a dry land. Women made up for it by using plenty of perfume. Scents were so popular that many people made a living making perfume.

Clothes were available to match your taste. Some were fancy and sold by merchants. Most were homemade but were sewn with special designs.

Girls probably played dress-up and put on their mother's clothes. They also enjoyed getting into cosmetic boxes and seeing how lovely they could be.

The average woman probably didn't spend too much time on her personal appearance, but we should not think she ignored it.

DETECTIVE CLUEDO

Case No. 17043

Crime:
Escaped prisoner

See how few clues you need.

Clue 1	Partner executed
Clue 2	Arrested by Herod
Clue 3	Refused to stop preaching
Clue 4	Believers prayed for him
Clue 5	Chained to two guards
Clue 6	Punched in his side
Clue 7	Chains fell off
Clue 8	Put on garment for cold night
Clue 9	Escaped to a Christian's house
Clue 10	At first not let in

Answer: *Peter* (Acts 12)

6-10 clues—You are a GRAND
　　　　　DETECTIVE.
1-5 CLUES—You are a SUPER
　　　　　DETECTIVE.

Case No. 17044

Crime:
Attempted murder

See how few clues you need.

Clue 1

Clue 2

Clue 3

Clue 4

Clue 5

Clue 6

Clue 7

Clue 8

Clue 9

Clue 10

A proud king

Made a ninety-foot golden statue

Demanded everyone bow down to it

Some Jews refused to bow to the statue

Three men refused

They were arrested

Trio were thrown into the fire

They did not burn

King saw a fourth man walking in the fire

King released the three men —
Shadrach, Meshach, and Abednego

6-10 clues — You are a GRAND
DETECTIVE.
1-5 clues — You are a SUPER
DETECTIVE.

Answer: *King Nebuchadnezzar* (Daniel 3)

Did you know?

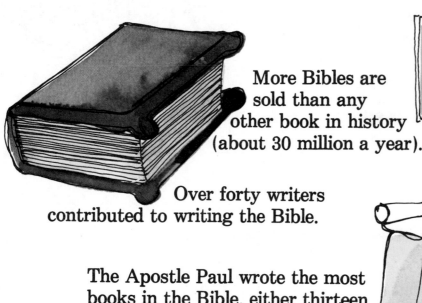

More Bibles are sold than any other book in history (about 30 million a year).

Over forty writers contributed to writing the Bible.

The Apostle Paul wrote the most books in the Bible, either thirteen or fourteen (Romans, 1 and 2 Corinthians, Galatians, Ephesians, Philippians, Colossians, 1 and 2 Thessalonians, 1 and 2 Timothy, Titus, Philemon, and maybe Hebrews).

The Bible has twenty-seven books in the New Testament and thirty-nine in the Old. How many all together?

Each of the first four books of the New Testament (Matthew, Mark, Luke, and John) is a history of the life of Jesus Christ.

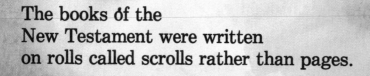

The books of the New Testament were written on rolls called scrolls rather than pages.

Most of the Old Testament was written in Hebrew. Most of the New Testament was written in Greek.

The word *Bible* comes from the Greek word meaning books.

King James had the King James Bible translated into English in 1611.

The first Bible in English was copied by John Wycliffe in 1382-8.

No book of the Bible has been written since 100 A.D.

DON'T SHAKE YOUR FIST.

That was King Jeroboam's big mistake.

The king was leading the people of Israel away from God. He had built a golden calf (an idol) and made sacrifices to it.

One day while the king was worshiping at the idol, a prophet of the true God came to him. The prophet warned him of God's judgment. As a sign that judgment would come, the false altar would soon split open and ashes would spill out.

King Jeroboam was furious. "Arrest that man," he shouted, and he shook his fist at the prophet. As he shook it, his fist froze into position. It was paralyzed so he couldn't pull it back.

At that moment the false altar cracked and ashes poured out. Jeroboam had made a big mistake.

(1 Kings 13)

The wicked grandmother

Most grandmothers are kind, loving, and sacrificing. Once in a while we hear about a terribly mean one. These stories make us glad for the good grandmother we have.

Athaliah (ATH-uh-LY-uh) was the daughter of two wicked parents, Ahab and Jezebel. They had worshiped false gods and killed many people in Israel.

Her son Ahaziah became king, and Athaliah taught him to be as evil as he could. Soon he was just as wicked as his mother and grandparents.

When Ahaziah was killed, Athaliah decided she wanted to rule. Immediately she had all of her grandchildren murdered. All except for Joash, her infant grandson, who managed to escape. His aunt smuggled him away.

Seven years later this young boy was made king. His grandmother Athaliah was killed for her wickedness.

(2 Chronicles 22,23)

Children didn't have electronic toys or motorbikes in Bible times. Their toys and games were simple and usually easy to make. Many of their games were much like the ones we have today.

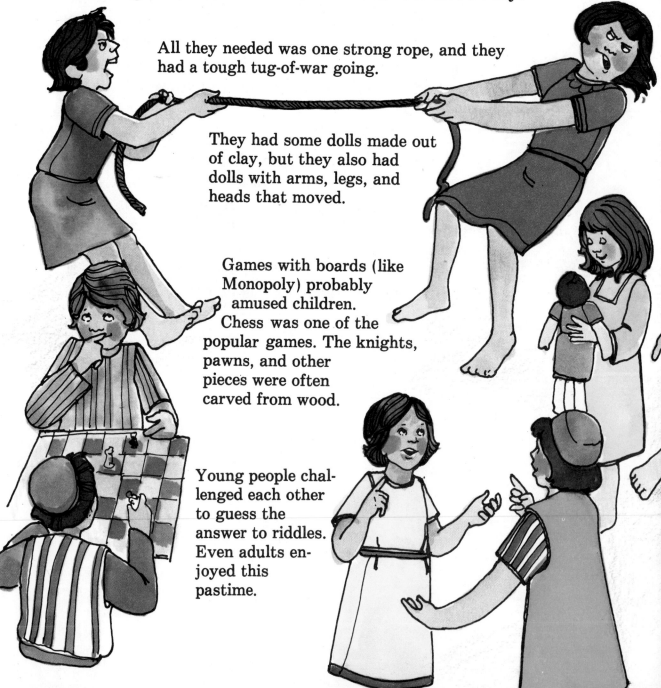

All they needed was one strong rope, and they had a tough tug-of-war going.

They had some dolls made out of clay, but they also had dolls with arms, legs, and heads that moved.

Games with boards (like Monopoly) probably amused children. Chess was one of the popular games. The knights, pawns, and other pieces were often carved from wood.

Young people challenged each other to guess the answer to riddles. Even adults enjoyed this pastime.

play?

Children invented all kinds of games with marbles. Sometimes players dug a row of holes in the ground. Standing eight feet away, they took turns tossing or rolling their marbles into the holes. Instead of glass, these marbles were either pebbles or joints from sheep's feet.

Boys and girls spent hours learning to juggle.

Blind man's bluff. Look out! This game could be dangerous. One player was blindfolded, and then slapped by other players until he or she guessed who was doing the hitting. Sometimes the players hit hard, and it hurt!

Hopscotch. A player, hopping on one foot, kicked a stone from one square to another. If both feet touched, the player was out.

Children have always enjoyed skits and plays. They would parade through the streets imitating weddings, military parades, and even funeral processions.

Toys and games have been found made from shells, ivory, gold, wood, and ebony. Jesus must have played many of these games as a child.

These people lived dangerous lives. Often they had to escape to save themselves. Can you match the person with the escape he used? If you get 5 out of 10, you can consider yourself an ESCAPE ARTIST. You will need to use some people twice. Number a piece of paper from 1-10 and write the correct number.

Moses

Joseph and Mary

David

Paul

Peter

Lot

Jews in Egypt

Spies at Rahab's

The People

Escape Artists

If you didn't get as many as you hoped, try this quiz again tomorrow and see what you have learned.

1. After he became a Christian, people wanted to kill him. He escaped at night over a wall in a basket.

2. An angel warned them to escape to Egypt.

3. Escaped death when his mother hid him by a river.

4. Hid in caves to avoid King Saul who wanted him killed.

5. Escaped from the walls of Jericho by climbing down a scarlet rope.

6. An apostle who escaped an angry mob with a Roman officer's help.

7. Escaped death by painting lamb's blood on door.

8. His wife helped him escape through a window, and then put a statue in his bed to pretend he was there.

9. Awakened by an angel and chains fell off in prison.

10. Hurried to mountains to escape destruction of Sodom.

Answers: 1.4 2.2 3.1 4.3 5.8 6.4 7.7 8.3 9.5 10.6

Is the Bible true?

Why do you trust a Bible written centuries ago? There are many reasons to believe the Bible is true. Look at just a few.

We know the Bible is true because of the promises it has kept. For instance, the prophet Micah said 700 years before Christ that the everlasting king would be born in tiny Bethlehem (Micah 5:2). Jesus Christ was born in exactly that town many years later (Luke 2:11).

As scientists continue to dig in old cities they find proof of Bible facts. Famous archaeologist Nelson Glueck says not one piece of historical evidence has ever been found that disagrees with the Bible.

We also know the Bible is true because it changes people's lives as it said it would. Many people have found new lives or given up terrible habits because they accepted the message in the Bible.

Maybe you have even more reasons for believing the Bible is true. There certainly are many reasons to trust what it says.

What is faith?

Faith is like a child sitting on a parent's lap. A child lays its head back, snuggles closely, and soon relaxes on a parent's chest. The child trusts his parent. He or she doesn't expect to get dumped on the floor, hit, or screamed at. Trust is at the center of faith. Since you have faith in God, you lean on him and relax.

(Hebrews 2:13)

Faith grows.

Your parents have prepared your meals and cleaned your clothes and hugged you for years. It's easy to trust them. The more you depend on God, the easier it becomes. Faith grows the more we use it.

(Luke 17:5-6)

Faith is believing in the unseen.

We don't have to see our parents in order to trust them. Your mother could be in the kitchen cooking, and you can't see her. But you feel good knowing she's around. Your father might be working in the garage or even at work. You don't have to see him.

We have faith in God without seeing him. We see the wind move the trees, watch plants grow, and talk to God. Faith means we don't have to see the person. (Hebrews 11:1)

Jesus believed it was easy for children to have faith in God (Matthew 18:2,3). Maybe that's because children practice by having faith in their parents.

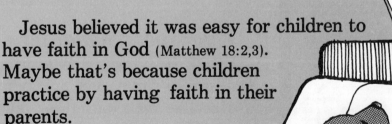

Miracles for children

Jesus healed children as well as adults. Several times the Bible says that Jesus Christ healed large numbers of people. Certainly, there were many children in these crowds.

At least four times, the Bible specifically names a child who was healed. Let's look at a quick description of those children.

Healing an official's son

A worried father traveled over from Capernaum to see Jesus at Cana. The father told Christ that his son was terribly sick. At any moment he might die.

The father asked Jesus to please come to Capernaum immediately. Christ told him to go home, because his son was already healed.

It was amazing. At the exact hour Jesus told him to go home the little boy was healed.

(John 4:46-54)

The rabbi's daughter

While Jesus was speaking, the local rabbi came over and bowed down. The man had great faith in Jesus Christ. The rabbi explained that his little daughter had just died. However, he was sure Jesus could bring her back to life by merely touching her.

When Jesus arrived at the rabbi's house, he took the dead girl's hand in his. Instantly she got up and was completely well.

(Matthew 9:18-26)

The girl had a demon.

Something evil lived in this little girl. It was called a demon, and it caused her to do strange things. Her mother loved her greatly and went to Jesus to see if he could get rid of the demon.

Jesus agreed to help the girl, and the demon left right away.

(Matthew 15:22-28)

The boy had a demon, too.

This young man was constantly hurting himself. He might fall into a fire and have to be rescued. On another day the boy slipped into the water and nearly drowned.

His father hated to see him bruised and burned and in daily danger of being hurt.

One day the father pushed his way through a crowd and knelt before Jesus Christ. He begged Jesus to heal his son.

Jesus asked the father to bring his son to him. When Christ saw the child, he healed him in a minute.

(Matthew 17:14-18; Good News Bible)

STRANGE FACTS

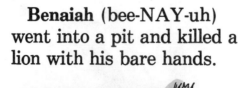

Benaiah (bee-NAY-uh) went into a pit and killed a lion with his bare hands.

Ishbi-Benob's (ISH-bii-BEE-nob) spear tip weighed over seven pounds.

The roof of the tabernacle was made of ram's skins, dyed red, and tanned goatskins (Exodus 26:14, Revised Standard Version).

A giant in the Bible had six fingers on each hand and six toes on each foot.

Zimri (ZIM-rii) was king of Israel for seven days. He had killed the previous king. When he heard people were coming to attack him, he went deep into the palace, set it on fire, and let it fall on him.

Rachel and Leah ate mandrake leaves because they believed it would help them have a baby.

Abraham was 100 and Sarah 90 when they became parents.

We often judge people in the strangest ways. Their size or looks become too important to us. David was turned down as king because of his appearance.

Samuel was sent out to select a king. He went right past David because:

Was David a ding-a-ling?

• David did not have a smooth face.

• David was too young.

• David was not tall.

God corrected Samuel. Later the small boy, David, killed the nine-foot giant Goliath. David became one of Israel's greatest kings. God knows better than to choose people by their appearance.

(1 Samuel 16:7, The Living Bible)

The following crimes have been committed. Your job as policeman is to arrest the correct criminal. Read the crime and description of the criminal. Select the guilty person from the list of suspects at the bottom of the opposite page. Be careful.

Number a piece of paper from 1-10 and write the correct answer by the number. If you correctly arrest 5 of the 10, you are a POLICEMAN; 6-8 makes you CAPTAIN OF POLICE; 9-10, and you are CHIEF OF POLICE.

1. *Wanted for baby killing*

Description: Suspect only killing boys. Has many thrown into Nile River. Handle carefully. Suspect sometimes believes he is more powerful than God.

Person you arrested

_____

(Exodus 1:22)

2. *Wanted for stealing*

Description: Former member of Joshua's army. Took gold, silver, and robes from Ai.

Person you arrested
_____
(Joshua 7:18-21)

ARREST THIS PERSON

3. *Wanted for ordering murder*

Description: Suspect has trouble making up his mind. Ordered innocent man put to death. Employed by Roman Empire. May frequently wash his hands.

Person you arrested

_____

(Matthew 27:21-24)

4. *Wanted for impersonating his brother*

Description: Suspect wore hairy skin to fool his father. Brother was tricked out of large inheritance.

Person you arrested _____

(Genesis 27:1-29)

5. *Wanted for murder*

Description: Had landowner murdered so her husband could have vineyard. Worships fake gods. Last regular employment was as queen.

Person you arrested _____

(1 Kings 21:1-16)

96

6. Wanted for murder

Description: Suspect murdered his brother after his offering was rejected. This was the first murder ever reported. Suspect wears a special mark.

Person you arrested

_____

(Genesis 4:1-16)

7. Wanted for stealing

Description: Former member of religious group. Likes to get job as treasurer. Suspect may have killed himself.

Person you arrested

_____

(John 12:4-6; Matthew 27:3-5)

8. Wanted for flight to escape serving God

Description: Last seen going away from Nineveh. Known to like boats. Check all ports. May be extremely close to a fish.

Person you arrested

_____

(Jonah 1)

ARREST THIS PERSON

9. Wanted for kidnapping

Description: Known to hate young brother. Brother was thrown into well and coat taken. Sold brother to a traveling group and told everyone he was dead.

Person you arrested

_____

(Genesis 37:12-35)

10. Wanted for escape from slavery

Description: Slave belonging to wealthy citizen near Colossae. May have stolen from owner. Last seen heading for Rome. Check with man named Paul who is living in that area.

Person you arrested _____

(Book of Philemon)

List of suspects: 1. Cain 2. Onesimus 3. Achan 4. Pharaoh 5. Judas
6. Joseph's brothers 7. Jacob 8. Pilate 9. Jezebel 10. Jonah

Correct criminals: 1. 4   2. 3   3. 8   4. 7   5. 9   6. 1   7. 5   8. 10   9. 6   10. 2

If you lived during the time of King David and you wanted to send four large packages from one city to another, what would you do? You would probably hire one of the trucks of the desert—a camel.

Camels are still used as trucks in many parts of the world. They are big, strong, and can travel many miles without water.

A camel's back stands about seven feet off the ground. They squawk loudly when they kneel down for loading. Over five-hundred pounds can be tied to them.

Fuel is no problem. A camel can go days without drinking and eat the toughest, most thorny of bushes. The hottest of days barely bothers him.

This animal carries refreshment for the driver, who often drinks camel's milk.

A camel's wide foot makes it ideal for racing across the sands of the desert. They can cover sixty-to seventy-five miles a day.

King David thought camels were so useful he hired a special Arab camel driver to take care of his camels. The Arab's name was Obil.

(1 Chronicles 27:30)

Why did he keep it a secret?

He was afraid of what would happen to him.

How did Joseph get the body?

He took a terrible risk and asked Pilate if he could bury Jesus' body.

What made him an open disciple?

Joseph did not want the body of Jesus Christ to stay on the cross over the Sabbath.

Who helped Joseph?

Nicodemus helped Joseph take the body down.

What did they do with the body?

They placed perfumes around the body and wrapped it in linen as was the custom.

Where did they put the body?

Joseph put Jesus in the tomb he had bought for himself.

Joseph could no longer be a secret follower of Jesus Christ. He loved Jesus so much he overcame his fear.

(John 19:38-42; Matthew 27:57-61; Mark 15:42-46; Luke 23:50-54)

101

If you pray for a new bike, will God answer you?

Yes! God will answer that prayer—one way or another.

First, you take your request to God and tell him exactly what you want. Be specific. While you are at it, tell him why you want a bike.

Now, look for God's answer. He will do what is the best for you and the people around you. That's one of the fantastic things about God. He sees the total picture and can make better decisions than we can.

God isn't a fairy godfather. He doesn't merely wave a wand and give us whatever we want. He isn't a genie who pops out when we rub a jar, ready to obey us. God is careful, thoughtful, and concerned about you.

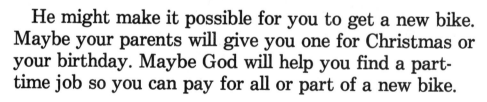

He might make it possible for you to get a new bike. Maybe your parents will give you one for Christmas or your birthday. Maybe God will help you find a part-time job so you can pay for all or part of a new bike.

Or, God might say "no." Maybe he will make your old bike run for a longer time. Maybe he will provide a way for you to get around without a bike.

When we ask God for something, we leave it with him. Any way he wants to answer the prayer is all right with us. But God will answer the prayer. And he will answer it as someone who loves you.

Can you live after you die?

Definitely!

We don't see people after they die, but they are still alive. Their body is buried, but the real person isn't.

Have you ever left some water in a jar in the hot summer? After a few days, the water is entirely gone. You can still see the jar. You can see the watermarks on the glass. But the water is gone.

What happened to the water? Did it stop existing? No. The water changed into vapor and now exists in the air. It is still around, but we can't see it.

Christians leave the body something like water goes into the air. We do it quickly. People on earth can't see us, but we are still alive.

Jesus told us that if we believed in him we would live in his Father's house in heaven. Jesus Christ lived, died, and rose from the dead so we could have this place called heaven.   (John 14:2; John 3:16)

The Apostle Paul told us we will some day have heavenly bodies. (Who knows what they might look like?)   (1 Corinthians 15:44-46)

There are many mysteries about death, but we do know that Christians go to live with God.

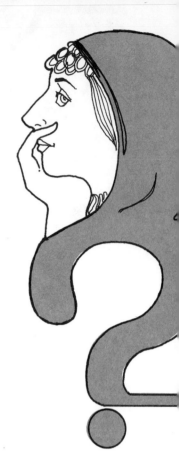

Selecting a Wife

How did your parents meet? There are many strange stories of how men and women selected their spouses. The Bible has some of the strangest.

See if you can match the couple with the way they met. A few of these are hard.

Couples

1. Adam-Eve   2. Jacob-Rachel   3. Isaac-Rebekah
4. Samson-Mrs. Samson   5. Herod-Herodias

How did they meet?

1. When he was forty, his father sent a servant to select a bride. This man had never met her until she became his wife.

2. His wife was made from his rib.

3. He wanted to marry a Philistine woman. His parents refused but later gave in.

4. This man married his brother's wife. A prophet objected to the marriage and was executed.

5. He worked for seven years to get his bride, but her father tricked him. He had to work another seven years (fourteen years in all) to marry her.

Answers: 1. Isaac-Rebekah 2. Adam-Eve 3. Samson-Mrs. Samson 4. Herod-Mrs. Herod 5. Jacob-Rachel

104

Can you match the mother with her famous child?

There are many famous mothers in the Bible.

If you get 4 out of 10, you are a PROFESSIONAL; 8 right makes you a SUPER-PRO.

Mothers

1. Sarah
2. Rebekah
3. Elizabeth
4. Mary
5. Eunice
6. Eve
7. Rachel
8. Hannah
9. Hagar
10. Bathsheba

Children

a. Jacob
b. Joseph
c. Jesus
d. Samuel
e. Solomon
f. Cain
g. Timothy
h. John the Baptist
i. Isaac
j. Ishmael

Answers: 1.i 2.a 3.h 4.c 5.g 6.f 7.b 8.d 9.j 10.e

Insults in the Bible

If you stick your tongue out at a person, it is a nasty insult. When you shake your fist, it means the same thing. There were insults during Bible times also. Here are just a few.

Ancient Israelites hissed at people they did not like. Hissing was like our booing. (Job 27:23)

BO-O-O

Hissss

Spitting at a person has always been an insult. So has turning your back on them. (Isaiah 50:6)

If you call people hypocrites, you mean that they are acting

If you shook the dust off your feet, it meant you did not like what a person was doing. You didn't even want to carry their dust with you.
(Matthew 10:14)

like they are religious when they really don't care about God.
(Matthew 23)

They called Jesus names.

What insulting, nasty names have you been called? Has anyone ever called you stupid, four-eyes, knucklehead, fatty, dummy, clod, or klutz? How about teacher's pet, idiot, or dense? Maybe you have been called something too nasty to write down.

It hurts to be called ugly names. Children don't enjoy it and neither do adults. Jesus probably didn't like it either, but people called him some mean names.

Jesus enjoyed a good meal like other people. His enemies called him a glutton even though he wasn't. That was like calling him a pig or fatty. He wasn't either one. (Luke 7:34)

Some of his enemies called him a drunk. The word was *winebibber*. No one ever saw Jesus drunk, because he never was. (Luke 7:34)

Many people in Judea hated the people of Samaria. Jesus tried to be a friend of the Samaritans. His enemies didn't like that, so they called him a Samaritan. They knew he was a Galilean, not a Samaritan, but they wanted to hurt his feelings.
(John 8:48)

His enemies also called Jesus crazy. They said he was demon-possessed. They were saying that Jesus couldn't control himself; instead demons controlled him.
(John 8:48)

We know what it is like to be called a nasty name. It hurts inside, it makes us sad, and sometimes we want to cry. Jesus knows how it feels, too. He can be a close friend when someone calls us an ugly name.

Were there sports in Bible times?

Sports events were big favorites during New Testament times. Thousands of people packed into large stadiums to watch famous and outstanding athletes. They didn't have baseball, football, or hockey, but the contests they did have took tremendous skill.

Wrestling was a big sport for both men and boys.

In a few places wrestling contests were held between animals and men. Usually the men did not do too well.

Running, discus throwing, spear throwing, boxing, chariot racing, and running in full battle armor were among the most popular sports.

It was rare for a valuable gift to be given. Most often the prize was a crown of leaves. They soon dried up, but the winner was proud.

If a young man won a contest, his family, friends, and community treated him as someone special.

Young men who wanted to try out for the Olympics had to keep two important rules. First, they had to promise to train for ten months. Second, they had to promise they would not cheat.

Paul often used sports to illustrate a statement he made. One such statement is found in 1 Corinthians: *"In a race, everyone runs but only one person gets first prize. So run your race to win."*

(9:24, The Living Bible)

His real name was Joseph. But his Christian friends nicknamed him Barnabas, which meant the "son of encouragement." They called him this because he enjoyed helping people.

Here are a few of the times he went out of his way to help others. Barnabas wasn't afraid to sacrifice.

• When the new Christians at Jerusalem needed food, Barnabas sold a field and gave the money to the apostles. They used it to help the families in Jerusalem.

(Acts 4:36,37)

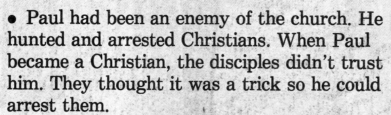

• Paul had been an enemy of the church. He hunted and arrested Christians. When Paul became a Christian, the disciples didn't trust him. They thought it was a trick so he could arrest them.

Barnabas believed Paul and accepted him as a real Christian. Because of Barnabas, the other Christians accepted Paul, too. (Acts 9:27)

Son of Encouragement"?

- When a new church started at Antioch, Barnabas and Paul went to teach the people.
(Acts 11:22-26)

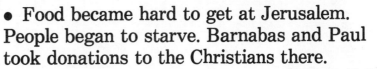

- Food became hard to get at Jerusalem. People began to starve. Barnabas and Paul took donations to the Christians there.
(Acts 11:27-30)

- One day Paul had an argument with Barnabas's young cousin, Mark. The apostle refused to take Mark on another missionary trip. Barnabas decided to take a chance. Instead of going with Paul, he asked Mark to go with him to Cyprus. (Acts 15:39)

These are just a few of the stories. Barnabas knew how to take chances and be a good friend.

The Word Doctor

These rhymes need help. What word would you prescribe to finish them?

To the blind man every day was night
Until Jesus came by and gave him
his _____
(Mark 8:22-26)

Lot's wife decided to halt.
She turned into a pillar of _____
(Genesis 19:15-28)

Martha and Mary were filled with gloom.
Until Jesus brought Lazarus out of the _____
(Luke 16:19-31)

When Jesus wanted a coin,
He didn't just wish.
He pulled one out
Of the mouth of a _____
(Matthew 17:24-27)

Mary and Joseph went on a trip,
They took Jesus to far off _____
(Matthew 2:13-15)

The Word Doctor

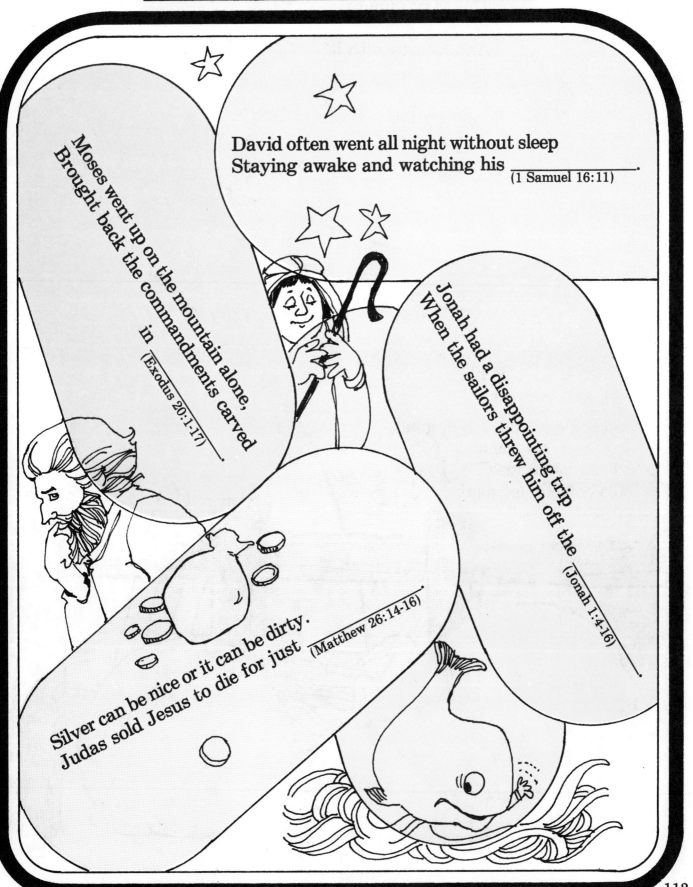

David often went all night without sleep
Staying awake and watching his _____.
(1 Samuel 16:11)

Moses went up on the mountain alone,
Brought back the commandments carved in _____.
(Exodus 20:1-17)

Jonah had a disappointing trip
When the sailors threw him off the _____.
(Jonah 1:4-16)

Silver can be nice or it can be dirty.
Judas sold Jesus to die for just _____.
(Matthew 26:14-16)

Answers: sight, fish, tomb, salt, stone, thirty, sheep, ship

Tell me now,
This very minute,
Who ate honey
And locusts with it?
(Matthew 3:4)

John the Baptist

Samson

There was a man who refus
to bend. Even when thrown
into a lion's den.
(Daniel 6)

Good-bye, my daddy,
Good-bye, my brother.
I don't like this place,
I'll find another.

But when money was gone
So were his friends.
Then he decided
To come home again.
(Luke 15:11-32)

The Prodigal Son

ople used to stop and stare
the things this person dared.
t the young man didn't care
e knew his strength was in his hair.
dges 16:1-22)

Thomas

Daniel

Judas

There was a man
Who wanted to meet
The person with holes
In hands and feet.

He stood stiff
With stubborn pride
Until he saw
The wounded side.
(John 20:24-29)

The Good
Samaritan

Tell me,
friend. Don't
be funny.
Who stole
the disciples' money? (John 12:6)

He was walking
bright and brisk,
Saw a man and took a risk.
Made sure the man didn't die,
While everyone else just
walked on by.

(Luke 10:25-37)

What is a disciple?

The word *disciple* is used over two-hundred times in the New Testament. It describes someone who learns from someone else. A baseball player could be a disciple of Fred Lynn, because he learns from him. A student could have been a disciple of Albert Einstein.

When a Christian is called a disciple of Christ, he is someone who learns from the Son of God.

Everyone may be a disciple of Christ. Our age makes no difference. We don't have to go to college or be a Christian for a long time. Every man, woman, and child can do it.

Jesus had twelve special disciples, called apostles, who were close to him. However, these were not the only ones who followed him and learned from him. Many others were called disciples.

If you would like to become a disciple, you must learn about Jesus Christ from the Bible and follow him by making your life like his.

Although it may be hard at times, it is exciting to live as a disciple. You are trying to live the life Jesus wants you to live. It is a feeling of helpfulness, kindness, and happiness.

A Secret Sign

Early Christians had a secret symbol. When they wanted someone to know they were Christians, they often drew a fish. Sometimes these were beautiful pictures. At other times they were easy line drawings like you and I make.

Paintings by Christians might have a fish in them. Often the markings on a grave had a fish to suggest the dead person was a Christian. Some churches probably had a fish drawn on the walls.

Today you will see some Christians wearing a pin of a fish on their clothing. Or see a plaque with a fish on it near the doorway of a house. Why a fish? Why not an eagle or a lion or a horse? There are probably several reasons.

The first reason is because there were five words of special importance to Christians:

The first Greek letter in each of these words spelled *fish*. (This is called an acrostic.)

But this isn't the only reason. Several of the first apostles were fishermen. When Jesus met them he said, "Follow me and I will make you fishers of men" (Matthew 4:18,19).

Jesus meant that the apostles would go out and tell people about Jesus Christ. They were "catching" them for the Son of God. They were "bringing them in" to understand and accept God's goodness.

Whenever a Christian saw the sign of the fish, it could remind him of two things. First, it meant Jesus Christ, God's Son, was Savior. Second, it reminded him of his need to tell others about Jesus.

Stones can laugh and dance if God wants them to. It's fascinating to see the miracles of nature in the Bible. Walls fall down, sticks grow almonds, and water turns to wine just because God wants them to. These are just a few of the stories.

The Rod Grew Leaves
(Numbers 17)

Moses told twelve men to each bring a rod. He said God would use the rods to show which man he had chosen.

All of the rods were placed in the inner room of the Tabernacle. The next day the rods were removed. The rod belonging to Aaron was different. During the night, this bare stick had blossomed—complete with leaves and ripe almonds. Everyone knew God had chosen Aaron.

The Jar That Wouldn't Empty (2 Kings 4)

A woman came to tell the prophet Elisha that her husband had died. Her two sons were to be sold as slaves to pay large debts. All the woman had for food was a jar of olive oil.

Elisha told her to borrow every pot and pan she could get. Soon her house was filled with them. She was then told to pour oil into each pot and pan.

The widow did exactly as she was told. Oil kept coming and coming. Finally every pot and pan in the house was filled. Only then did the jar run dry.

The widow sold the oil, paid all of her debts, and had enough

Nature did

more funny things

money leftover to support both her sons and herself.

The Walls Collapsed on Signal (Joshua 6:1-20)

Sometimes walls fall down. But how often do all the city's walls collapse at a signal?

That's what happened at Jericho. General Joshua marched his troops around the city for seven days. Then the troops blew trumpets and shouted. At that moment the walls of Jericho tumbled down. Joshua's soldiers poured into the city and easily won the battle.

Water Turned to Wine
(John 2:1-11)

Jesus was at a wedding when they ran out of wine. His mother begged Christ to solve the problem. He may not have wanted to at first, but he agreed.

Six large pots of water were brought in. Each held fifteen-to-thirty gallons. When Jesus told them to dip water out, it had already turned to wine.

The Talking Donkey
(Numbers 22:21-38)

Someone was waiting to kill Balaam. His donkey knew about the danger and decided to protect him. The donkey pressed close to a wall to avoid the trouble. But Balaam's foot was crushed.

Balaam didn't know his life had been saved, and he was furious. He beat the donkey three different times.

Finally the donkey spoke. "What have I done?" he asked.

DETECTIVE CLUEDO

Case No. 17045

Crime: Famous thief

See how few clues you need.

Clue 1	From Israel
Clue 2	Old Testament character
Clue 3	Member of an army
Clue 4	Sent to investigate country
Clue 5	Helped lose army battle
Clue 6	Stole clothes and money
Clue 7	Worked for Joshua
Clue 8	Spied on city of Ai
Clue 9	Stolen goods burned
Clue 10	Suspect stoned to death

6-10 clues—You are a GRAND
DETECTIVE.
1-5 clues—You are a SUPER DETECTIVE.

Answer: *Achan* (Joshua 7)

Case No. 17046

Crime: Idol building

See how few clues you need.

DETECTIVE CLUEDO

Clue 1 Had famous younger brother

Clue 2 Lived before David

Clue 3 Israel's first high priest

Clue 4 Helped Moses lead the Hebrews out of Egypt

Clue 5 With Israel in wilderness

Clue 6 Grew tired of waiting for Moses to return from Mount Sinai

Clue 7 Collected golden earrings

Clue 8 Made golden calf

Clue 9 Led Israel to worship idol

Clue 10 Did not enter the Promised Land

6-10 clues—You are a GRAND
              DETECTIVE.
1-5 clues—You are a SUPER DETECTIVE.

Answer: Aaron (Exodus 4-32)

Index